TRANSFORM YOUR PUBLIC SPEAKING

TRANSFORM YOUR PUBLIC SPEAKING

Nina Valentine

CLAREMONT BOOKS

PENGUIN BOOKS

Published by the Penguin Group
Penguin Books Ltd, 27 Wrights Lane, London W8 5TZ, England
Penguin Books USA Inc., 375 Hudson Street, New York, New York 10014, USA
Penguin Books Australia Ltd, Ringwood, Victoria, Australia
Penguin Books Canada Ltd, 10 Alcorn Avenue, Toronto, Ontario, Canada M4V 3B2
Penguin Books (NZ) Ltd, 182–190 Wairau Road, Auckland 10, New Zealand

Penguin Books Ltd, Registered Offices: Harmondsworth, Middlesex, England

First published by Penguin Books 1993
Reprinted with minor revisions 1994

This edition published by Claremont Books,
an imprint of Godfrey Cave Associates Limited,
42 Bloomsbury Street, London WC1B 3QJ,
under licence from Penguin Books Ltd, 1995

ISBN 1 85471 766 9

CONTENTS

ACKNOWLEDGEMENT

Permission to use the extract, which appears on page 35, from George Orwell's 'Politics and the English Language' has been kindly granted by the estate of the late Sonia Brownell Orwell, and Martin Secker & Warburg Ltd.

INTRODUCTION

Increasingly there is a need for everyone to learn public speaking skills, for speaking in public does not mean simply standing on your feet and delivering an address. You are speaking in public whenever you make a statement on behalf of an association to which you belong; whenever you are interviewed on radio or television; whenever you move a motion at your club; whenever you are asked to be a spokesperson for any group of people; whenever you move a vote of thanks; whenever you propose a toast at a function; and whenever you take part in a debate. As well as that, you might feel passionate enough about a subject to *want* to make a public speech about it.

All these facets of speaking before the public are covered in this book. The qualities of a memorable speaker are catalogued and examples given of good and bad practices. The preparations needed for a memorable speech are outlined, as well as ways of adapting to the needs of your audience. There are hints about how to cope with a microphone. Performance on radio and television is discussed in detail. The rules of debate are set out in Chapter 11, and Chapter 16 discusses forms of address for prominent citizens.

Make a careful study of the book's contents and you will become a confident, interesting speaker who has something to say and who is listened to with respect.

1 KNOW YOURSELF

'All the great speakers were bad speakers at first.'
Ralph Waldo Emerson, 1803–1882

No one is born talking. We all learn – admittedly some better than others. But however expert we are, we *learn* to speak. And we can all learn to speak in public. It is an acquired art, not an innate ability.

AN ESSENTIAL SKILL

Increasingly people need to know how to express themselves publicly. Representatives of clubs, union members, witnesses to events, players of sport, winners of awards, experts in all sorts of fields, and parliamentarians – they all need to know how to put words together to make an harmonious whole.

Sadly, it is not a skill taught in many schools. Teachers are hell-bent on educating their students to write well, but only a handful of students receive intensive training in speaking in front of others. Yet in job interviews, for example, answering questions face to face is top of the priority list. Few future employers will give a prospective employee a list of questions to be answered on a form; they will want to converse with the applicant to judge whether that person will be capable of filling the role in question.

Displaying confidence

Nervousness can take over in this situation and the job may be lost simply because it is so difficult for an applicant to say exactly what she or he wants to say. If there has been a good deal of practice in speech, in verbal communication, this kind of nervousness won't happen. The applicant is relaxed and therefore able to present as a confident person, quite capable of doing everything the position demands.

Applying for a job is, of course, only one situation where good, confident speech is vital. There are so many others. Just saying something in front of other members of a club to which you belong can become a nightmare if you do not have the confidence to express yourself appropriately and clearly. Indeed, speaking aloud anywhere has its hazards. Listening to or watching interviewees on radio or television can be enlightening. The hesitation with which many people answer questions, and the embarrassment that shows in a person's voice or body language, can be quite nerve-racking. All this comes back to the lack of confidence felt in this confronting position. Being accustomed to listening to your own voice will overcome all that nervous tension, and will ensure that you present yourself in the very best possible light wherever you might be and whenever you are called upon to speak.

PRACTICE

No one will pretend that speaking in public is easy. It can be hard indeed to change your attitude to this very public arena.

Nervousness can stop you from even trying. The old adage of 'Try, try again' applies here. Practice will help. The more you speak, the better you will become. You will be able to feel it within yourself, for you will know when you have expressed your thoughts in an interesting way and when you have engaged the sympathy of your audience – one or two listeners, or one or two hundred. Or thousand! Let's assume that you have made up your mind to accept this challenge of speaking in public, and you want to know how to go about it. The first step is to know yourself.

2 WHAT TO DO

'I have learnt a good deal from my own talk.'
Thomas Chandler Haliburton, 1796–1865

First of all you will need to listen to yourself. Consciously listen to what you say.

FINDING YOUR FAULTS

Do your statements always make sense? Are you saying *exactly* what you mean to say? Are you using the dreaded 'er' and 'um'? Is your voice too high-pitched for others' comfort? Do you gabble? Do you speak too slowly? Are you fluent, or hesitant? Are you boring in your speech patterns? Do you use far too many clichés? Do you speak much too softly? Too loudly? Are you repetitive? Do you listen to what others are saying? Do you answer questions precisely? Are you always succinct?

Heavens, but you *are* a mess!

WORKING ALOUD

Having listened carefully, you can identify the problem or problems and begin to work on them in the privacy of your own home, aloud. You must listen to yourself becoming better. Inside your head will not help at all. You must listen to yourself as others hear you, for only then will you improve.

You do not need expensive equipment to listen to yourself. Of course if you have recording equipment at home it is good to use it. Playing your speech back can be a salutary experience! Re-recording and listening again will be very helpful – or should be. But it is possible to listen to yourself much more easily. Simply cover one ear and then speak aloud. Your voice will sound different, as though it is in an echo chamber. That is how others hear you. With such an easy method you can listen to yourself anywhere. Each time you listen to yourself, go through the mental checklist of your shortcomings as a speaker. Try to do something about them, so that you really sound the way you want to.

MAKING CHANGES

It is not easy to change the way you sound. Your voice is so much part of you that you may not wish to sound any different. That's fine. But consider this – there could well be something in that litany of speakers' faults that does apply to you and your speech mannerisms.

If you do decide to change, to improve, do it gradually, until the new sound becomes part of the natural 'you'. Heaven forbid that you should sound elocutionary, because in all public speaking the aim is to sound natural and spontaneous.

NERVES

After all this listening, you still feel nervous? Let's do something about that too, because if you are to give your best you must not *appear* nervous. You can be nervous inside, but you must seem confident to your audience, large or small. So deep breathing is called for, deep breaths from your diaphragm.

Don't gulp air into your lungs, raising your shoulders, for that will result in shallow breathing that simply adds to your panic. When you have expanded your lungs properly that extra oxygen will calm the fluttering feeling in your stomach and your voice will stop shaking. You'll feel much better.

There's another trick you'll need to know. Tell yourself that other people have coped with this situation. They have no more talent than you do. If they can cope, so can you. You'll show them, and yourself, just how a speech ought to sound. Of course you will not be satisfied with your first few efforts, but as you improve you'll find that you get a real buzz from speaking. It can be exciting, rewarding and fulfilling. It can also add to your self-esteem, and that's no bad thing.

BREATHING

We breathe automatically; but for speaking in public you need to learn to breathe in a particular way. This can be achieved by some simple exercises that will expand your lungs and allow you to take in more oxygen than you might do normally. This will settle your nerves. More important, it will give you extra voice power, extra control and extra projection. You'll need that when you are speaking for any length of time in a large room.

Use your diaphragm as a singer does, to strengthen the muscles around it to hold the windpipe's column of air as it presses against the vocal chords. Daily stand erect, with your hands meeting across your diaphragm, fingers just touching. Breathe in slowly and deeply, forcing your fingers apart. Hold your breath for as long as you can without discomfort. Allow the breath out slowly and evenly. Do this up to 20 times a day and soon you will begin to notice a great improvement in the length of time you can sustain this outflow of breath. When you think you have improved sufficiently, begin to count with the outflow of breath. Start with five or six, repeating the numbers slowly, then gradually extend the count. After two or three weeks you should be able to reach 20 without any undue strain. It sounds too easy to be effective, but it does work. No more shakes, no more running short of breath, no more shattered nerves. Just one thing: persevere. It's well worth it.

A cautionary tale

There is a wrong way of breathing, which will actually make you more tense. This is called clavicular breathing. The term is used because in this type of shallow breathing the collarbones and shoulders are raised. The upper chest is surrounded by a rib cage that cannot be expanded very much at all, so at that point lung capacity is restricted. The short supply of oxygen you get from clavicular breathing will produce a loud hail or a shouted command quite effectively but it will be of no use when you need to give a sustained speech in a large space.

To recognize the *wrong* way of breathing, just gulp in some air as though you have been running hard and need a quick supply of air to your lungs. Notice that your shoulders are raised while you are doing this and that there is some resultant tension in your throat and neck muscles. This is what will cause you to suffer a mild form of panic – not recommended for a controlled performance.

So out with the wrong and in with the right: use your diaphragm for correct, deep, satisfying breathing. Exercise this large muscle each day by doing the breathing exercise described above, until you can feel it acting as a bellows to pump large amounts of air into your lungs. Then, and only then, will you be ready to think about the voice itself.

YOUR VOICE

Now the voice is so much a part of you and your speech that it must be a voice you can produce well. You must also like the timbre of your voice. It is the musical instrument each of us carries about with us and it is possible to improve it.

Find a passage you would like to read aloud. Do that without being too dramatic in your interpretation. Give full worth to each word and try to read it with good sense, as the writer would like you to do. Either record the passage or listen with one ear firmly blocked out.

If you do not like the sound of your own voice, accept that, but also accept the fact that you can do something about it. If it is too soft, increase the volume; if it is too loud, decrease the volume. If the timbre is too high, take some time to exercise your voice at lower registers. Say aloud several times each day: 'Roll on, thou deep and dark blue ocean, roll'. Start this in your ordinary voice, then repeat it on a lower register and then lower still until you reach the level that pleases you. After much practice you will discover to your delight that this tone is now normal.

If your voice is too dull you will need to work on it for some time, consciously injecting each reading with light and shade, with variety of tone and speed, until you like the flexibility you have achieved.

Really this improvement is up to you, for only you can get your speaking voice the way you want it. It will take time and it will take some effort, but like so many things the reward will be worth it. *You* will notice the difference and be pleased by it. When that happens your confidence will soar. With that new-found confidence comes the wish to show it off. And you will show it off, the very next time you are asked to speak anywhere before others. After all that thought and work it will be a good experience.

Checklist: what to do

- Listen to yourself
- Work on the problems identified
- Conquer your nerves
- Improve your breathing
- Avoid wrong breathing
- Improve your voice
- Exercise to lower your voice tone

3 QUALITIES OF A GOOD SPEAKER

'I pass like night, from land to land: I have strange power of speech.'
Samuel Taylor Coleridge, 1772–1834

The qualities of a good speaker are numerous, but all of them can be acquired by diligence and practice.

A good speaker needs:

- a carrying voice
- a confident appearance
- a well-researched subject
- a smile
- the ability to appeal to an audience
- a sincere approach
- fine use of language
- the power of persuasion
- the knack of speaking *to* listeners and not *at* them
- precise timing
- self-control
- an attention-gaining manner
- an easy progression of ideas
- a sense of audience reaction
- a knowledge of how to adapt to a particular occasion
- clarity of speech, so the audience understands each word
- vitality in presentation of ideas
- a genuine desire to communicate.

THE DETAILS

It seems a tall order, but rest assured it is attainable. Let's take each quality and look at it in more detail.

A carrying voice

Well, there's not much point in speaking if no one can hear what you are saying. So pitch your voice about three quarters of the way down the length of the room or hall and you'll find it will be easily heard.

Confidence

If you exude confidence your audience will relax and prepare to enjoy the event. It will also mean that your air of confidence rubs off on you and that, no matter how nervous you might really feel, no one else will know. You will be able to carry off the occasion with aplomb.

Research

This one is really self-explanatory. It is necessary to know your subject thoroughly. Research or experience or both does this for you. The idea of delivering a speech or even a short talk on a subject in which you are not competent is the stuff of nightmares!

Smiling

A smile will win your audience every time. Make sure it is not a fixture, particularly if the subject is a serious one, but do use your smile to draw your listeners. There are dozens of small muscles around your mouth and when you smile they relax, giving you confidence as well as encouraging your viewers to like you and your appearance.

Appeal
You need to appeal to the sensitivities of your listeners. This means that you touch them in some way, relate to them so that they want to listen, want to understand your message. To do this you need not harangue them, but reasonably put your case, develop the theme of your speech, inform them, and if possible entertain them too.

Sincerity
This is perhaps the most important quality for good public speaking. A lack of sincerity can be picked up very easily. There is nothing quite so chilling to an audience as this, for they feel they are wasting time and being hoodwinked by an 'expert' who is no such thing.

Use of language
Try to use language that says exactly what you want it to say. Don't waffle about looking for the right word, larding your delivery with 'ums' and 'ers'. Just say succinctly what you need to say, in words your listeners can easily understand. Try to choose colourful language that will paint word-pictures; this means that those images will stay with the people who hear you. It will mean that you have achieved your purpose because what your language has depicted is deemed memorable.

Persuasion

Your powers of persuasion need to come into play when you are speaking in public. Very often you will be hoping to convince your audience of a particular viewpoint. If this view is unpopular you will certainly need to express yourself well and in persuasive language. Do remember to refute any arguments contrary to your point of view, so that no doubts are left in the mind of your audience.

Speaking *to* your audience

When you are delivering a speech, develop the technique of speaking as though you were addressing one person. This will ensure that you are speaking *to* your listeners and not *at* them. A hectoring manner never goes down well with listeners. They cannot relate to this *manner,* so they tend not to listen to the *matter.* If this happens, there is no point in your being on your feet at all. It is the difference between hitting someone over the head with a blunt instrument to gain your point and negotiating by argument and subtle persuasion.

Timing

This is vital to the success of your speech. If you are asked to address a group of people and you are given a time limit of fifteen minutes, you should stay within that limit. Over time is usually boring time.

Time your speech carefully during preparation. If it is too short, add to it. If it is too long, prune it. You will discover that this means your speech is more appealing, for you have cleared away a deal of dead wood and refined your arguments. You now have a clarity of vision you did not have when you were raving on for thirty minutes. It is always better to have your listeners wanting to hear more than to have bored them rigid so that the very mention of your name brings back that feeling of 'When will this end?'.

Self-control

You should be able to restrain your feelings when you are in public. This does not mean that your own enthusiasm ought not to be on display. It does mean that you should not break down, even if the topic is a very emotional one. Usually an audience is left with the memory that you cried, but the reason for this emotion is seldom remembered. Your aim is to inform an audience or to persuade them to a particular course of action, not to allow your own feelings to take over and ruin your presentation.

Attention-gaining

Don't creep out when your name is announced. Walk confidently from your position on the stage or in the audience. Stand up confidently if you are to speak from the floor at a meeting. Don't be apologetic. After all, you have prepared for this event, you know what you want to say, and you know that you can say it well, so there is nothing to be frightened about. Your opening statement will gain attention immediately, so that you can sail on from there, happy in the knowledge that you are being listened to and appreciated.

Progression of ideas

If you do not plan your speech well and have your notions running off at tangents, your listeners will find it extremely difficult to follow you. You need to have one idea leading to another in a steady progression. This logical introduction of subjects pertaining to your theme means a responsive reaction is assured.

Audience reaction

Recognising the reaction of an audience comes with practice, but you need to understand it if you are to be a good public speaker. No two audiences are the same; for example, a successful appearance before a small well-informed group will not necessarily be duplicated before a large group more ignorant of your topic. If people begin to shuffle, if they cough constantly, if their eyes seem to glaze over – you are in trouble. You have not gained their interest.

If this happens, you have some choices. You can cut your speech short and sit down before total disaster strikes. If it seems that your listeners are not understanding the words you are using, discard the exotic and speak in simple terms. You will see their expressions change the moment they are understanding what you are saying. If you try to introduce humour and they are not laughing, drop that tactic and try another.

Endeavour always to have a good rapport with your audience, for only if you *have* endeavoured will you feel that inner glow of satisfaction that comes with a well-prepared, well-delivered speech. You need to experience that every bit as much as your audience needs to be informed or entertained or cajoled or taught or stimulated – whatever the aim of your address is.

Adapting

Adapting to your listeners' needs is not easy, especially if they seem to want something you are ill prepared to give. You simply must try. Using language well, you can create an atmosphere of trust that will finally win them over. But it takes time, and you may not feel that you can afford this luxury. It is far better to adapt your thoughts to those of your listeners than to plough on, leaving them behind! Always consider them and always aim to have them with you rather than against you. Keep your own style, but always adapt that style to suit the particular occasion.

Clarity

It is vital that you are understood. To make sure of this, be certain that your voice is clear, your words suit your audience, that your volume of production is correct, and that you clearly pronounce each word you utter. No consonants missing from the ends of your words, vowels given their full measure, and correct pronunciation of any tricky words. If you are not sure of a word, leave it out. Substitute another easier word with which you are familiar. This saves embarrassment to you and to your listeners.

Vitality

This may seem like a strange quality to include in this litany of desirable qualities, but when you think about it you will realise that it is necessary. A lack-lustre performer will give a lack-lustre performance that satisfies no one. A vitality and a willingness to be there on your feet, speaking, are crowd-pleasers. An expressive face that mirrors your pronouncements is a wonderful asset. That also comes back to vitality and to personality. Project your sincerity and your warmth and you will be surprised at the positive reaction this achieves.

Communicating

Communicating through speech begins in the cradle and does not finish until the deathbed. What happens in between is up to you. The reasons for communicating in speech are complex, and they serve different purposes.

- A news broadcaster has one purpose, to inform.
- A radio university course is there for a teaching tool, as is an exercise programme or a cooking programme.
- A political broadcast is used to persuade.
- A variety show or a play is for entertainment.
- A documentary is intended as a stimulation – a starting-point for discussion – in speech.
- Interviews may be for instruction or for entertainment, or for both. Children's programmes answer both these purposes.

You, as a speaker, have a burning desire to communicate, but when you are planning your speech it would be as well to make up your mind just which category is yours. If you can inform, teach, persuade, entertain, stimulate and instruct all at one time in one speech, then you are at genius level. Aim high and you might approach this. Getting near it is a most satisfying trip.

Of course your topic will determine how you go about the planning process, and whether you feel you can be entertaining or informative. Be aware that you need to be aware and all will be well.

SOME 'DONT'S'

As a speaker, *don't*:

- speak unprepared
- be apologetic, particularly about lack of preparedness
- ignore a structure and simply ramble on
- learn your speech by heart and then recite it
- be so married to your notes that you can't introduce something topical for a particular group of people
- mumble
- speak so quickly that your listeners can't follow
- speak so slowly that they are nodding off between sentences
- speak in a monotone
- harangue
- give lengthy statistics that will bore everyone witless
- quote without giving your source
- patronise your listeners
- over-use slang expressions
- use jargon, or acronyms unless you are prepared to state what the letters stand for
- be repetitive, unless you know it to be essential

- be superficial
- over-talk (less is beautiful in this instance)
- tell off-colour jokes
- keep your eyes on your notes, instead of on your audience
- slouch
- sway from side to side (your audience will be mesmerised, and follow you)
- display mannerisms (taking glasses off and on constantly, for example, can irritate your audience)
- thank your listeners at the conclusion of your address (they should thank *you*)
- exceed the time limit.

It's a fearsome list, and you will probably be able to add to it. Simply think back to one of the most boring speakers you have heard and categorise the faults. It will be a sorry list, but it will be a good lesson for you as you set out for success in this most public of arenas.

Checklist: qualities of a good speaker

- Good carrying voice
- Confidence
- Research
- Smile
- Appeal
- Sincerity
- Good use of language
- Persuasiveness
- Address one person
- Good timing
- Self-control
- Attention-gaining techniques
- Ideas progressing naturally
- Gauging audience reaction
- Adaption to needs of the audience
- Clarity of voice
- Vitality of personality
- Communicating appropriately
- List of 'don'ts'

4 YOUR APPEARANCE

'The sense of being well dressed gives a feeling of inner tranquillity.'
C.F. Forbes, 1817–1911

~~~~~~~~~~~~~~~~~~~~~~~~~~~~~~~~

Appearing in public is *very* public. That is why you must be certain that you are comfortable in the clothes you wear on these occasions. You do not want to be over-dressed, nor too under-dressed. You should be making the best of yourself and that means wearing the clothes that most become you.

CLOTHES AND CONFIDENCE

Your clothes should also give a feeling of inner confidence. If you are worried about an ill-fitting suit, for example, you will be conscious of your discomfort. That will detract from your address. Your mind should be totally focused on what you are saying; it should not be distracted by the thought that you should have worn another outfit altogether. Think about the occasion, think who is likely to be there, and decide on your clothing. Then forget about it.

COMFORT

Get directions for the conveniences before you go into the venue, or before your speech time. How can you concentrate on your carefully constructed speech if all you want to do is go to the lavatory? While you are there, make sure that you look in a mirror. Look at your hair. If you are wearing make-up, check it.

It's really a matter of common sense. Your inner comfort, your own feeling that you look right, the knowledge that you have prepared your self as well as your thoughts, will enable you to deliver your talk with assurance.

FORMAL OR INFORMAL?

This will depend upon the occasion. Of course if you are the guest speaker at a formal occasion and the invitation states that it is formal, then you will dress accordingly: for women a dinner gown and for men, 'black tie' (a dinner suit or dinner jacket). People still judge by appearance to some extent, so conforming to the required standard of dress is simply sensible. If you are not sure, err on the side of formality. This will then be interpreted as a desire to please your listeners, for they will see that you thought it was an event worth taking some trouble about. Paying a compliment to your audience in this way always gets you off on the right foot. That first impression is still important.

Don't wear a hat unless it is a tiny unobtrusive affair. A hat will shade your eyes, the most expressive part of your face, and will create a barrier between you and your listeners. For the same reason don't wear you hair in a floppy, unmanageable style. Not only will this hide your eyes, it will also lead to annoying mannerisms as you shake it back, or hook it back, or fiddle with it.

In general, present yourself neatly and attractively, so that your listeners can grasp your appearance instantly, like what they see, and then forget about it. After all, you don't want them concentrating on your odd socks or fussy scarves or jangling jewellery or egg-stained tie instead of on your words and your vital message, do you?

WHAT TO DO WITH YOUR HANDS

No one seems very conscious of hands until standing before an audience. They then become the worst appendages of the human body. They don't seem to fit! *The Devil's Dictionary* defines a hand as 'a singular instrument worn at the end of a human arm and commonly thrust into somebody's pocket'. When you are performing in front of an audience, the last place for your hands is in your pockets.

So where do you put them?

- If you are speaking from behind a rostrum, rest your hands lightly on it. Don't lean heavily on the rostrum; this will give you a bad posture and make you look and feel tense.
- If you are speaking from notes, have them in the hand natural to you and hold them at about waist level. You can then grasp your wrist with the other hand and appear perfectly relaxed throughout your speech.
- If you are speaking without notes it is acceptable to lace your fingers together lightly and hold your arms in front of you. Hands loosely hanging at your sides really do look rather awkward from the audience.

- One hand may be hidden behind your back, where it can behave as nervously as it likes while from the audience you appear calm and poised.
- Don't fold your arms or stand arms akimbo. This looks as though you are gossiping, and is really much too sloppy to be acceptable.
- Of course you may want to use your arms (with their attached hands) to gesture while you are talking. This is fine so long as you don't overdo it. Aim to use a variety of movements during your address, but don't be too sudden in any of them, for they can be too startling, leading to a reaction from your audience you don't want.

STANCE

Don't stand stiffly. You will look nervous and inexperienced. One foot a little in advance of the other will distribute your weight evenly. If you need to change position slightly, do so by transferring your weight from the ball of your foot. If you use your heel it will be obvious to your audience that you are uncomfortable.

If you are given a table or a rostrum you are not obliged to use it, though it often helps. You can use it as a prop – or as concealment for your shaking knees!

If the rostrum is too high, stand to one side of it, rest your notes and one hand on it, make yourself comfortable, and speak from that position. If a microphone on a stand is with a too-tall rostrum, ask to have the microphone moved and lowered to your height, and ignore the rostrum altogether.

If the table is low, just rest your notes where you can refer to them, resist the temptation to lean over, and give your speech from the side.

THE EXTRAS

You are the guest for this occasion, and you should be made to feel special, and given every consideration. Making sure that the extras provided for you are correct is very important. Microphones can be temperamental. The same applies to an overhead projector or a slide kit: have it tested and make sure it is working, as you do not want any hiccups to spoil your carefully prepared address. Even if you have to arrive early and do the checking yourself it is wise to do so, for what suits one person does not always suit another.

Checklist: your appearance

- Be comfortable with your choice of clothes
- Check your appearance before going into public view
- Err on the side of formal dressing
- Control your hands
- Stand easily
- Ensure that any extra equipment works

---

5 ADAPTING TO YOUR AUDIENCE

'And as time requireth a man of marvellous mirth and pastimes; and sometimes of as sad gravity: a man for all seasons.'
Robert Whittinton, born c. 1480

A woman or man for all seasons is an adaptable person, one who can change direction if necessary to please a group of people. Careful preparation will not always prepare you for a hostile audience, nor even for a wildly enthusiastic one. It is up to you to adapt your style and your subject matter to the occasion. It will come with practice, as does so much else connected with speaking in public.

BE SINCERE

The greatest weapon in your armoury is sincerity. When you are speaking to a group that you know does not agree with your viewpoint, that sincerity will win you respect and maybe some converts. Your knowledge of your topic is also vital, for it is impossible for you to change anyone's outlook if you are not steeped in the theme of your address.

ASSESS YOUR AUDIENCE

The second aid for you is an assessment of the assembly. Are they older than you expected? Younger? All female? All male?

Well or ill educated? Perhaps even well primed? Having made that assessment you must decide how you intend to adapt your subject matter once you are on your feet. Scribble yourself a few extra notes to guide you on your altered path, and then try to please as many listeners as you possibly can. You cannot deliver a successful speech if you are not fully aware of your audience and its needs. To give your listeners satisfaction and pleasure is your aim, and if you concentrate on that, and not upon gratifying your own ego, you will be a much better performer.

You cannot be all things to all people, but you should try.

Be certain that the language you use is understood. There is little point in using words an audience cannot interpret. If you are in doubt, then the better known, usually shorter word is the one to use. Remember Winston Churchill's 'blood, sweat and tears'? Nothing could be more simple, and nothing could be more memorable.

NEVER SPEAK DOWN

The young audience and the old audience need to be treated as people, not as people in special categories. Speaking down to children or being coy is not to be countenanced. Shouting at the elderly because the assumption is that they are deaf or stupid – or both – is inexcusable.

Of course you may need to speak a little more slowly and a little more distinctly if you see some of the gathering straining to receive you, but don't overdo it. They will follow you and appreciate you in exactly the same way as any other group of people – with the innocence or wisdom of their years perhaps more so. Being sentimental or condescending to either group is unforgivable.

CONSIDER YOUR AUDIENCE

Your listeners are all-important to you, for they are the reason you are there delivering this address. Adapt your style, your vocabulary, and your message so that it matches their capacity to understand you. Be interested in them and they will be interested in you. It is as basic as that. You can't have a sea of satisfied faces looking back at you at the conclusion of your speech unless you have given them something to be satisfied about. Have you informed, entertained, cajoled, taught or stimulated them by your words and actions?

Whatever your aim was, if you can feel satisfied that you have fulfilled it to the best of your ability you deserve that glowing vote of thanks. Smile and accept it.

Checklist: adapting to your audience

- Adapt your style and subject to the audience
- Always show sincerity
- Choose shorter words rather than longer
- The young and the elderly are people
- Be interested in satisfying your listeners

---

6 CHOOSING THE BEST LANGUAGE

'Don't quote Latin, say what you have to say, and then sit down.'
Duke of Wellington, 1769–1852

~~~~~~~~~~~~~~~~~~~~~~~~~~~~

The spoken word is very different from the written word. Once an idea is written down it may be referred to again and again. It will have time to seep down into the consciousness, to be absorbed. There is no such luxury with the spoken word. Because of this, all speakers ought to think carefully about their choice of words.

You should make sure that they are colourful, meaningful, and apt for the occasion. Painting word-pictures well gives your listeners an impression to take away with them. If you are making a direct statement and supporting it with your research or knowledge you will have much more impact from the rostrum. Going around the point instead of coming to it directly is to be avoided at all costs. Your choice of words is paramount for doing this effectively.

FIT THE WORDS TO THE PEOPLE

Never aim your vocabulary below the intelligence of your listeners, but discipline yourself to use words that will be easily understood by all attending. This is vital for success. You want to communicate your ideas; that is the reason for your being where you are, so your words must convey your meaning.

SLANG, JARGON AND CLICHÉS

Avoid slang or jargon unless it is essential to a story or an illustration you are using. Jargon is particularly irritating. Every profession has its own form of spoken shorthand, understood by its members but not understood by others. Gardeners use Latin names, engineers speak incomprehensibly about stresses, doctors can make a stomach ache sound like a subject for intensive care, and all organisations use abbreviations meaningless to those outside that specific group. Don't indulge in jargon from the public platform. It will only confuse, and if you are desperately trying to make a point you will destroy your chances of doing so.

Don't use clichés – worn-out phrases that have been heard so often they are without impact. Find another way of describing calm than by referring to a millpond; and a different way of saying 'dead as a dodo'. Other creatures are just as crazy as loons; plainness does not always have to be connected with the nose on your face; and a sore thumb is often not conspicuous at all.

CHOOSE GOOD WORD-PICTURES

Be original in your choice of vocabulary, especially of descriptive words, and you will get your message across much more interestingly. Here's an example to help you. 'I am typing this manuscript on a nice new typewriter, sitting in a nice room, with a nice bowl of flowers on the table before me. I have just enjoyed a nice cup of tea and am looking forward to a nice dinner this evening'.

How much better it would have sounded if I had told you: 'I am typing this manuscript on a new electronic typewriter, sitting in a sunny room, with a bowl of autumn flowers on the table before me. I have just enjoyed a cup of lemon tea and am looking forward to a grilled chop for dinner this evening'.

You now know a great deal more about me than you would have done if you had heard only the first statement. 'Nice' is a word that has lost all meaning, for it describes nothing accurately any more. Be adventuresome in your word choices and you will be rewarded with much more interested reactions than you thought possible.

You have not bored your listeners – you have given them something to think about on a simple subject because you have painted them a clear picture of a domestic situation. Some of the information imparted will stay in the mind of the listener.

AVOID TANGENTS

A memorable speech is a logical speech. One idea leading to another is easier to grasp when it is the ear only that is engaged. Flying off a topic with tangential ideas is fine for ordinary conversation but is not acceptable for a speech. Stay on the line you have set yourself, and take your listeners with you along that path. In this way they will relate to you and your theme.

When you have to compress your thoughts to fit into a set time you will discover just how valuable words can be. The right words used in the right places in your speech will give exact meaning to your sentences. You have had to precis and refine what you planned to say, and in that way you have cut out the waffle. Extraneous words are so unnecessary you'll wonder why you ever included them. Over-speaking is really a crime. Punching firmly on those words you need to get your message across is the answer.

THE KEY PHRASE

Introduce a key phrase throughout your address if you think it appropriate. Come back to it again and again. Emphasise the meaning of the words until you are sure that even the least informed member of your audience has grasped your point.

If you are to use this method the words must be apt. Think of advertising slogans that you have remembered well. They all have few words, but they are words carefully chosen to convey a message. Because they are so right you remember them effortlessly; but without that hard work and that exact word choice you would never have done so. It ought to be the same with your planning. Select words for the meaning you want, and whack your listeners over the head with them if necessary. Do anything you have to to make your words memorable.

THE NEW WORD

If you have found a new word that you like and want to use, make yourself familiar with it beforehand. Try it out in normal conversation until you are comfortable with its usage. Only then may you use it in public. If you trot out that new word for the very first time before a group of people, they will know that you are not too sure of its meaning – or even of its pronunciation. It will fall flat and so will your credibility. New words that extend your vocabulary are marvellous and to be encouraged, but not at your expense.

Use your dictionary, enjoy the challenge of your discovery, and only then share it with others.

ORWELL'S ADVICE

Almost fifty years ago George Orwell set out six rules governing the use of good English. These were to apply to the writing of English but they are equally applicable to spoken English. They are worth pondering.

(i) Never use a metaphor, simile or other figure of speech which you are used to seeing in print.

(ii) Never use a long word where a short one will do.

(iii) If it is possible to cut out a word, always cut it out.

(iv) Never use the passive where you can use the active.

(v) Never use a foreign phrase, a scientific word or a jargon word if you can think of an everyday English equivalent.

(vi) Break any of these rules sooner than say anything outright barbarous.

It is easy to see that if you do follow these rules your speech will be concise, appropriate, full of punch, original, and easy to follow. You could not ask for anything better than that.

WORDS ARE YOUR TOOLS

Eliza Doolittle in *Pygmalion* confessed to being sick of words. That will never do for you. Words are your tools of trade. Cherish them, use them wisely, make them your friends and you will find you are ever more interesting to those around you and to any group you are called to address.

In *Alice in Wonderland* Lewis Carroll had Humpty Dumpty say scornfully: 'When I use a word, it means just what I choose it to mean – neither more nor less'. Humpty Dumpty's philosophy was to use words as power tools. Follow that example.

Checklist: choosing the best language

- Think carefully about your choice of words
- Use an understandable vocabulary
- Avoid clichés
- Choose original descriptive words
- Strive to be logical
- Cut out extraneous waffle
- Try out a new word before using it publicly
- Memorise George Orwell's list for good English

---

7 THE USE OF HUMOUR

'A joke's a very serious thing.'
Charles Churchill, 1731–1764

If you can make your listeners laugh they are likely to be receptive to what you say. Don't overdo it, however; a speech larded with jokes and anecdotes can actually be boring. The important thing is to choose humour carefully so that it is appropriate.

YOUR JOKES MUST FIT

If you have decided that your speech will be an entertaining, amusing piece, then fine; go right ahead. Dredge up every joke you can, and leave your audience rolling in the aisles. Even then you must be certain that you have not contrived the humour. It must fit within the framework of your speech and fit snugly. Seamless humour is the right humour. The speaker who begins with, 'A funny thing happened on my way here ...' and then drags in some fanciful story that bears no relationship to the topic or the occasion or the members of the audience, is not a speaker to invite again. The speaker who smiles happily some way into the address and relates an anecdote that dovetails exactly with the subject matter and the professions of those listening, is the speaker who has done her or his homework. That is the guest you will want to invite again.

NEVER EMBARRASS

Humour is one of the most effective tools for any speaker to use, but is must never be an embarrassment. Think carefully before including humour, and before deciding to plan an amusing speech. Wrongly handled, humour is a double-edged sword; it can cut the giver as well as the receiver.

Think about your particular audience. A risqué story might go down well at a sportsmen's dinner, but would fail to raise a smile at a Women's Institute meeting. Too many mistakes of this kind will damage the reputation of a speaker and will have the listeners squirming in their chairs. Humour can be offensive in many contexts, so it needs to be handled cautiously.

Sexist and racist jokes should never be included in a speech.

THE FIZZER

If you have told a joke you think highly appropriate to the occasion and to your listeners and it falls flat, just ignore it and go on with the rest of your speech. After all it's not so very important; it is one ingredient in the dish of your making. The rest of the recipe will be as apt as when you prepared it. Make a mental note not to use that story again. You are, we hope, planning and preparing to become an appreciated public speaker, not a stand-up comedian.

A TALENT TO AMUSE

An original amusing incident woven into your speech (perhaps from some personal experience that ties in beautifully with the theme you are attacking) will bring a smile to everyone's lips. That's what you aim for, not a reaction to an outmoded joke, a stale story, an off-colour comment, crude use of language, or a cartoon caption everyone has read in the morning's paper.

Entertaining with humour will also relax you as a presenter, so it is important to use this effective weapon as often as you can. But do not contrive to use it – contrived humour never works. It adds nothing to the matter under discussion, and leaves you with a very uncomfortable feeling.

Checklist: the use of humour

- Never contrive to introduce humour
- Choose jokes carefully
- Personal anecdotes can be relevant
- If a joke falls flat, ignore it and continue
- Be entertaining, but not at any cost

8 PLANNING A SPEECH

'In Maine we have a saying that there's no point in speaking
unless you can improve on silence.'
Edmund Muskie, 1914–

~~~~~~~~~~~~~~~~~~~~~~~~

So where do you begin? At the beginning, of course: think about
your subject. If you have been given a free choice be certain
that you select a topic that is familiar to you, one on which you
can speak with conviction and enthusiasm. If you have been
given a theme, think of what you know about it; then discover
where you can find more information and how you can make it
personal to your experience.

THE BONES

When you feel happy about your topic, sit down and note a few
points in a broad framework. You need an opening statement
that will arrest the attention of your listeners immediately; you
need to grab their interest, hold it as you develop your
argument, and then leave them with a conclusion that makes a
strong impact. So they are the bones on which the flesh of your
speech will rest: opening; development; and conclusion. The
greatest challenge lies in your concluding sentences, because
they will make your speech memorable or – heaven forbid –
instantly forgettable.

PLAN FROM YOUR CONCLUSION

Often it is more difficult to finish than to start. Bearing this in mind, try writing your final words first and then work backwards. In this way you will find that you really do have something to say. You are not just talking. You are working from your worth-while conclusion, gathering your information and your points as you go. Anecdotes will suggest themselves to you and if they are relevant to the subject matter you are preparing they will lighten, or illustrate, that matter.

THE OPENER

You have your framework and your ending, so now for the beginning. Often it will arise from the conclusion, and thus will make a whole upon presentation. That's good. If it doesn't work that way, think of a stimulating question to use as an opener: 'Do you know that the lilies of the field ...?'; 'How does you garden grow?'; 'Do you consider that women have wasted their votes?'. Something like this will have you launched into your speech in two seconds flat, and because of the pertinence of your question you will have gained the attention you seek.

FIRST WORDS

'Mr (or Madam) Chairman, ladies and gentlemen' are always the first words you say when you are facing your audience. This is the correct procedure, but it also gives you a chance to breathe deeply, look about you, quickly assess your numbers, gauge the pitch of voice you will need, and to smile. You are relaxed (or appear to be), your listeners relax. After that, you hit them with your carefully prepared opening sentence.

Play safe

If you have a varied audience and wish to include numbers of people in your opening gambit, do so at your peril. Unless you have a *complete* list in your hand you will be bound to miss someone. That is a disaster, and ought not to happen.

The Mayor may be there, however, particularly if you are to address an annual meeting, and she or he ought to be included. Simply add 'Madam (or Mr) Mayor' after your acknowledgement of the person in the chair.

Don't add anyone else; you will be embarrassed for ever if you omit a name you should have remembered. The general opening statement is all that is necessary.

WHAT NEXT?

The body of your speech is next. You have your opening and your conclusion. Experienced speakers will sometimes tell you that the rest will take care of itself. It often does, but only after years of practice.

Plot your speech

Your planning strategy is now to plot the course of your speech by noting its progression. Let's take an example. You are a noted gardener and you have been asked to speak about your own garden. You have your opening: 'How does *my* garden grow?'. Now sit down with a pad and pencil and note down just how it does grow.

- With difficulty.
- To a yearly plan.
- Colour variation.
- Maintenance of lawns.
- Pruning of trees.
- Open days.
- Satisfactions.
- Tasks still to complete.
- Conclusion (A poem? Quotation? Picking up the first thought?).

Let it simmer

If you have time, let the subject simmer for a few days and add or subtract ideas as they come to you. Your original list may not look anything like the completed one, but so long as you are satisfied with it and can speak to it, that is all that matters.

Expand on the difficulties of growing exotic plants in a cold climate, the horror of weeds, the constant raking of leaves. Mention how all year round you plan your tasks in the garden so that you have time for other hobbies too. Talk of colours in your flower beds and why you have chosen those tonings. Give some insight into the maintenance of velvet lawns and the annual pruning of the trees that grow there. Refer to the Open Days you have initiated to raise money for charities (perhaps the one you are speaking to, so mention that if it's relevant).

List the satisfactions of your work in the garden, and the joy it gives you to share its beauty with others. Describe the plans you have to transform that acid-soil corner into a ground-cover exhibition, and the long-range plan you have for replacing the hedges with roses.

Look for a poem or quotation relevant to your topic. Choose one that you think will have an impact on your listeners; perhaps Prince Charles' 1980 statement, 'To get the best results you must talk to your vegetables'. Place it for maximum effect, perhaps right at the end.

When all this planning has been lodged in your consciousness for some time, talk it through to yourself. When you think you can follow your notes easily, time what you are saying.

Time to the minute

Timing is vital. You want to fit within the time limits you have been given. You want to leave them longing to hear more from you. You were asked for fifteen minutes and you are taking nineteen. Don't be tempted to leave it all there. Chop out four minutes! No one will know except yourself that you have made this sacrifice. Perhaps leave out the yearly tasks; many of them will be covered in other areas you can talk about anyway. Your satisfactions and your Open Day could be amalgamated, and save you another precious minute or three.

However you do it, *cut to the time limit*. Time really is of the essence. It is much better to have a satisfied audience interested in your fifteen-minute talk than one bored rigid because you spoke for thirty minutes with padding and waffle.

THE OCCASION: THINKING ON YOUR FEET

The time has come. You are about to present your speech.

You are now aware of your own capabilities, you have worked on your breathing, your voice and your nerves, you understand the 'don'ts' for a public speaker, you have told yourself that you are confident, you have checked your clothing, you know how to stand and where to stand, you have chosen to include some subtle humour in your speech, you have rehearsed your well-chosen language, you have planned your delivery carefully and you have timed the whole thing exactly. You are ready.

You have been introduced, you have risen to your feet and positioned yourself behind or beside the lectern. Your notes are resting exactly where you can see them easily, you take a deep breath and say: 'Madam (or Mr) Chairman, ladies and gentlemen ...' You are off!

Look at your listeners

Your speech is being well received, but suddenly you sense that you are losing the interest of your audience. What could be wrong? Probably this is happening because you are not connecting directly with your listeners. Nerves, which you thought you had under control, are keeping your eyes down on your notes. You must raise your head and actually *look* at your listeners. Your eyes are the windows of your soul, the most expressive part of your face, and you must focus them upon your audience for maximum impact. You have rehearsed your speech, you do know what is to come, so you can afford to look at all those people who are there especially to hear what you have to say.

Modify your delivery

You could be losing your rapport with the audience because your voice is too soft. Lift its volume and you could notice a difference instantly. If that doesn't remedy the situation, try slowing the rate at which you are speaking. It is very difficult to listen to someone who is racing along; the mind just cannot keep up with the spoken word if the rate is too quick.

The other reason might be that you have fallen into the trap, also brought on by nervousness, of speaking in a sing-song monotone. This will put your listeners to sleep very quickly. You can't hold their interest if they are slumbering – and if they are snoring it can interrupt your thought processes very badly indeed!

Vary your presentation, inject light and shade into your voice, make a startling announcement, and that should do the trick.

Of course you have to do all this while you are still speaking, so it is not easy. Don't worry about it. It will come with practice, as will so much else in this field of endeavour.

A minute to go

It is almost the end of your speech. You have checked your watch and discovered that you are on the fourteen-minute mark. Fine; one minute to go. But you have not used all your notes. Too bad. Don't be tempted. Mentally take a leap to your final rehearsed thoughts. Share a few of those notions and then announce your final summation in that sentence you have prepared previously. That should have them all applauding. If they have not realised that you have indeed finished, just smile at them all and sit down or step back from the lectern.

Don't say, 'Thank you' or even worse, 'Thank you for listening to me'. That will spoil the effect of your last statement and rob you of your triumphant closing. Your listeners ought to take home with them in their minds that final ringing sentence. It can be something humorous (if, and only if, it is appropriate), a provocative statement designed to have everyone thinking, a sentiment to stir the heart or a succinct summing up of the arguments you have presented. Whatever it is, make sure it is not likely to be forgotten. On their way home you want your listeners to be discussing your speech – favourably.

AFTERWARDS

When the event is behind you and you have found that you enjoyed it, take some time to evaluate your feelings.

- Why did you enjoy speaking in public?
- Would you repeat the experience if offered the opportunity?
- What did you gain from it?

Knowing the answers will make you a better performer.

Get an opinion

Ask someone you knew in the audience to sum up how she or he felt about your speech. Ask about the presentation, your voice, the matter you included, the reaction that person had to your arguments or to your information and whether you were considered sincere. Of course not everyone will tell you the exact truth, but it is worth doing, for there will be some responses from which you can learn.

Review your performance

Go back over the occasion. Did you speak at a good pace? Did you pitch your voice towards the back of the venue? Did you emphasise the words and phrases you wanted to, so that your points were clearly made? If you are not quite satisfied with those areas, work on them as you rehearse your next address. You can be your own best critic. Until you are satisfied, you will not be able to give of your very best.

You will know instinctively when you have reached a peak. Once there, aim to stay at that pitch and to enjoy the experience of speaking even more.

Checklist: planning a speech

- Think about your topic carefully
- Find a startling beginning
- Try working backwards from a stunning conclusion
- Minimise references to individuals in your formal opening
- Plot the course of your speech in note form
- Expand those notes
- Time to the minute
- Monitor your presentation
- Traps to avoid
- Don't conclude with 'Thank you'
- Think about your speech afterwards
- What areas can be improved?

9 CONDENSING A SPEECH

'I dreamt I was making a speech in the House. I woke up,
and by Jove, I was!'
Duke of Devonshire, 1835–1908

There is an enormous difference between reading to the public
and speaking to the public. If you write out your speech and
then read it from the podium you are about half as effective as
if you speak from notes. As a beginner it is usually best to write
your thoughts out clearly and then rehearse from them at home.

THE SCRIPT

We've all seen politicians and public figures read a speech
without deviating from their script at all. This is boring to listen
to and boring visually. Often you see the top of the speaker's
head and nothing else: no eye rapport, little change of expression,
absolutely nothing to give the listener any joy.

Resolve to do much better yourself. It is not so hard as it
might seem at first sight. Write out your speech by all means,
but then dissect it to discover the highlights.

YOUR NOTES

Put down the highlights on a small piece of card. If you need
several pieces (especially at the beginning of your ascent),

number them boldly; you don't want to lose your place up there in public view. Write on one side of the card only, for there is less chance of losing your thread this way. When you are speaking you will slip each used card behind the others as cunningly as you can, and then refer to the new one.

With everlasting practice you will become much more expert, and will need only one card to trigger off your rehearsed memory of what to say and (often) *how* to say it.

Clever cues

The notes are for your eyes only, so don't be afraid to underline key words, tell yourself to slow down, note that you need to emphasise this phrase, write in a pause if you think it necessary – anything at all that will make your delivery more potent.

Try not to be too reliant on your notes. They are not meant to be used as crutches; they are the means by which you get your message across with maximum effect. By looking at your listeners, secure in the knowledge that your notes have been well prepared, you will be able to involve them much more than if your head is down as you read from a script.

Use them boldly

Don't be ashamed of your notes. Use them openly, especially if you are quoting something. And when you need to refer to them, bring them up to your sight line; don't bend down to consult them, thus cutting yourself off from your audience.

Just in case . . .

Of course there may come a time when you feel you do not need notes to help you. You are speaking on a topic so dear to your heart that you do not need any reminders. Fine; do that. A word of warning, though. Have those notes in your handbag or pocket *just in case*. A bad attack of the nerves could succeed in blanking out all thoughts for a time, and those precious notes will get you back on the track again.

Nothing can take the place of really thorough preparation, but these tiny reminders will serve as the keys to your gems of wisdom.

Discarding the prop

Think of your notes as the trainer wheels on a two-wheeler bike. They are there to aid riders until they can ride alone. They are not meant to be a prop for ever. Once you have the confidence to discard the extra wheels, you ride more freely and easily and can cover greater distances.

The same will apply to your speaking in public. Once you can discard writing your full speech, and then your notes, spontaneity will be easier. The difference will startle you, for you will have thus progressed from being a fine speaker to an excellent one who is in demand. Once you are in action your thoughts will flow, the reaction of those people listening to you will be more positive, and you will have direct eye contact. It's a heady feeling. It leads to a better presentation and a more satisfying occasion for everyone.

Checklist: condensing a speech

- Dissect your long speech
- Makes notes to remind you of your thoughts
- Use a small piece of card
- Write on one side only – clearly
- Use your notes to help your delivery
- Remember that notes are not crutches
- Work to discard notes altogether

10 SHORT SPEECHES

'Let thy speech be short, comprehending much in few words;
be as one that knoweth and yet holdeth his tongue.'
Ecclesiasticus 32:8

~~~~~~~~~~~~~~~~~~~~~~~~~~~~~

In your life as a public speaker you will make more short speeches
than long speeches. You'll be asked to make introductions,
move votes of thanks, or propose toasts. To do all those things
properly you'll need some guidelines. It is important to know
what to do and how to do it. So this is a chapter to read and
note carefully.

INTRODUCTIONS

Introductions have one purpose: to introduce the speaker to
the audience. They are not a vehicle for the person asked to
make the introduction to air her or his own views, or share long-
winded recollections of the guest when they were fellow-
students in kindergarten.

Speeches with this purpose should be short but to the point.
Double-check the title of the person you will be introducing
(see Chapter 16). Always check that you have the name of the
speaker correct. Nothing is worse than to have someone say:
'Miss ... er, Dr ... um ... I do beg your pardon!'. Pronounce the
name correctly, too. Check this with the speaker first, even if
the name has a customary pronunciation (for example I am

always pleased when I'm introduced correctly as Nina with an 'i' sound). Then practise the pronunciation until it comes naturally to you, using phonetic spelling or some mental rhymes if that helps.

Check the subject matter, too. It is rash to assume that because you've earlier heard Mr Butcher speak about the meat trade that he will do so again. Usually these matters can be resolved in the few moments before you are on your feet to make the introduction.

The form

Something like this would be ideal:

Madam Chairman, ladies and gentlemen: it is a pleasure to have Mr John Smith with us this evening. Mr Smith is a Fellow of the Royal College of Surgeons. His books on the subject of bone structure, and on his other great passion, the saving of our environment, are well known. It is a privilege to have him as our speaker on this occasion. How he intends to do it I do not know, but he assures me that his address will combine bones and the rainforests. Ladies and gentlemen: Mr John Smith.

You have mentioned the name, you have given her or his qualification for being at that particular event, you have conveyed something of the subject of the address, you have involved yourself and your audience and you have finished with the person's name. Correct, mercifully short, and pertinent. When the name of the speaker is mentioned right at the end the applause should begin, so that the guest is able to take her or his appointed position on a warm tide of approval.

Keep it low-key

Whatever the situation, say nothing to detract from the speaker. If you must share an anecdote about your guest keep it apt and short. The person who is to speak is the subject of the introduction – not yourself. You are merely the vessel by which the information is to be given to the audience. And if you have decided to mention anything more about the topic, do make certain that the speaker wants to share that particular part of the speech beforehand. Otherwise you may unwittingly give away the very point the speaker was planning to keep as the climax of the address. Check this detail in those few moments you have before the speaker rises to begin the address. It is much better than making a fool of yourself and ruining the surprise element carefully planned by the guest.

THANKING A SPEAKER

There are some schools of thought that believe this practice is overdone. Not so; from the content of the earlier chapters you can see how much thought and preparation goes into the making of a successful speech. Surely the person who has done this, who has shared information and has entertained you, should be thanked for the effort?

Make it spontaneous

The very formal vote of thanks is now seldom heard, and that is probably a good thing. It did tend to be so stiff that sincerity was lost in the formality. Thanking a guest speaker is a spontaneous speech: you cannot prepare it all beforehand. It must be graceful and short, referring to the speaker and what has been said. Listen for one outstanding comment made from the platform and refer to it. This will prove to the speaker that at least one person has been awake during the talk! Something specific also makes it easier to be sincere and to express your gratitude.

An example

Let's imagine that the speaker has been addressing you on the topic 'Women's Rights Today'. Somewhere in the body of the speech the speaker has cited Germaine Greer as an example of a forthright woman who has made an impact on society. In your thanks you could include something like this: 'When Germaine Greer's *The Female Eunuch* was first published few of us thought that she would become the household word she is today. We are grateful to you for reminding us of her forceful impact on women's rights'.

Begin your speech of thanks with 'Mr (or Madam) Chairman, ladies and gentlemen', and conclude it with 'Please join me in showing your appreciation of . . .'

The poor speaker

And if the speaker has been a poor one? What on earth do you say? You include the fact that the speaker has shared her or his thoughts with you and has made the time available in a busy schedule to be with your group on this occasion. Thanks can be expressed for this with very little reference to content that might accurately be described as dreary.

An effort has been made, and you should acknowledge it. A good speech of thanks reflects this commitment and good manners demand that you express appreciation as well as the circumstances permit.

Don't debate

No person thanking a speaker should argue with the speaker, or make corrections to a speech, or use the occasion to push out a barrowload of ideas contrary to that of the guest. That is just bad manners. It is a public opportunity to say 'Thank you' sincerely for the time and the work that has been put into the preparation and delivery of the speech. Even if you passionately disagree with the philosophy of the speaker you do not say so. You might be permitted to say '... it has been a controversial address that will give everyone who has heard it a great deal to think about ...' That is very different from vehemently opposing all that the guest speaker espouses.

Be brief

Say your few words in a sincere manner, making appropriate, specific reference to the address and, after a genuine, warm appreciation of the event, *sit down*. It is not the place of the thanker to make another speech. Sufficient to have one – and a good one – at any function.

PROPOSING A TOAST

There are many occasions at which toasts are drunk. This means there are many occasions at which someone is asked to propose a toast. You are lucky if you are warned before the event. More often than not in these informal days someone will suddenly say, 'Oh, Aunty Betty will propose the health of Kim'. When this happens there is no need to panic, although with some warning you might well have fulfilled the task superbly. Impromptu speeches can still be excellent.

Prepare in a second

While the company are settling to listen take a few moments to think of Kim in a positive manner. Remember one or two occasions (not embarrassing ones) in Kim's life, and then rise to your feet. You do not have to speak for very long, but you need to say something that the family and their friends will *remember* afterwards. The vital thing is actually to propose the toast. Many people forget why they are speaking and sit down with a sigh of relief, only to be reminded that they have not said the magic words ' ... and now will you join me in raising your glasses to drink a toast to ...'

Keep it light-hearted

Weddings, baptisms, birthday parties, retirement gatherings, and all similar occasions will have some toasts drunk. As they are usually light-hearted events, the proposer should try to keep the toast light-hearted too. Uncle Jani who goes on and on reminiscing about three past generations is not the person to ask to propose a toast at any family celebration.

If you are choosing someone to propose a toast, ask a person who is close to the heart of the matter but who has a light, amusing touch. The toast will then be handled in the way you would like it to be.

Three minutes is plenty

Generally a toast should not last longer than three minutes, preferably two. That is quite long enough for the speech itself and for the charging of glasses at its conclusion. Often at social functions guests are standing, and they do not want to be kept on their little flat feet longer than is necessary. Remind yourself of this before you begin speaking. In this way your speech preceding the toast will be crisp, accurate, and appreciated by those listening to you.

Loyal and patriotic toasts

These toasts are in a class of their own. For a **loyal** toast (that is, to the reigning British monarch), usually the chairperson simply says, 'Ladies and gentlemen, the Queen'.

Patriotic toasts are usually drunk at dinners connected with the armed forces. They are simple too; for example, 'To Her Majesty's Forces'. If a reply to such a toast is called for it must be brief, particularly if the Army, Navy and Air Force are all present and all feel constrained to say something.

A good rule for replies on these occasions is: 'Be brief, be sincere, and be seated'. It's not a bad rule for *all* toasts and replies.

OPENING SPEECHES

You might be called upon to open an art exhibition, a school
fete or a conference. What is called for on this occasion? The
first requirement is, as for all other speeches, some thought well
in advance of the date. You need to know something about the
exhibition, the fete or the conference.

■ Who is organising it?
■ Why have you been asked to officiate?
■ Who will benefit from the money raised or the purpose of
  the function involved?

When you have ascertained the answers to these questions, set
down a plan of action for yourself.

You cannot plan to make a long speech because on the day
everyone is longing to get on with it; often children are racing
around; people may be standing; and sometimes it is difficult to
hear the speaker, particularly outdoors. So give yourself four or
five minutes at the outside, and be strict with your timing.

A simple plan on paper should be something like this.

1 Opening remarks. (Thanks to introducer? Glad to be here?)
2 The organisers and the good work they do.
3 Your association with this group ... the reason for your
   attendance.
4 Anecdote tied to the event?
5 Raising money important ... continuing work ... give
   generously.
6 Declare the function open.

Don't forget the last item in the list. The late Dame Zara Bate was opening the Ballarat Begonia Festival some years ago. She made a short and interesting speech and sat down. She had to be reminded that she was there to open the Festival. With laughing apologies the deed was done, but it is best to remember it first time round. Most people at that opening would not remember Dame Zara's speech, they would simply remember that she forgot to declare the Festival open!

If you follow this basic structure you will be able to open anything at all.

MAKING A PRESENTATION

You have been asked to present the award to the best speaker in the Orators' Competition. At such an august gathering you must do your best, so again a plan is called for.

1 Your thanks for the introduction.
2 Your commendation of the contest's organisers.
3 Importance of such training, and high standard of contestants.
4 If award has been named for someone, for example the Peter Ustinov Cup, brief mention of why he was chosen.
5 Your reason for being asked to make the presentation.
6 Name the winner.
7 Present the cup: 'It gives me much pleasure . . .'

Any presentation following these principles will go easily and well. If there is no real contest involved just leave out the references to the standard of competition.

REPLYING TO A PRESENTATION

If you win a competition you will be called upon to make a reply to the presentation. It needs to be short and sincere. Give it a little thought before the day if you think you have a chance of winning, and you will be sure to do it gracefully. If there are several people who contributed to your success, put their names on a piece of paper. Take that with you and have it handy when your name is announced. There is nothing worse than thanking three people when it should have been four! Remember to thank the organisers of that particular event, and if there has been a corporate sponsor include that name too.

The conclusion might be a statement about the future of the awards and a few words of encouragement for next year's aspirants.

TWO IMPORTANT 'NEVERS'

In prepared or impromptu, in long or short speeches, *never* apologise for lack of preparation and *never* indicate when you are about to finish.

If you apologise you will make your audience uneasy, for you are signalling to them that you are about to make a poor speech. They will judge you from that standpoint, so you actually begin with your listeners against you. That makes it harder to win them over, and you don't want that.

If near the conclusion of your address you say, 'My final point ...' or 'In conclusion ...' or 'Lastly ...', you will be deafened by the sighs of relief, the rustling of papers, the opening clasps of handbags and the muttered 'about times'. In short, you will have lost the attention of your audience. This will not do: in their relief they will miss that summing up you have slaved over.

When you are near the end of your address, you are the only person who knows. Keep it that way. Lead up to the last statements and then hit them solidly between the eyes with that rehearsed last sentence.

After they have been stunned by your cleverness and convinced by your arguments they can prepare themselves for the ordinary. Not during that last brilliance.

Checklist: short speeches

- Keep introductions short and apt
- Say nothing to detract from the speaker
- Thank a speaker sincerely
- Thank a poor speaker graciously
- Don't argue with a speaker's viewpoint
- Proposing a toast at a family gathering
- Loyal and Patriotic toasts
- Opening a fete, a conference or an exhibition
- Making a presentation
- Replying to an award
- Never apologise
- Never announce the conclusion of your speech

11 DEBATING

> 'I love argument. I love debate. I don't expect anyone
> to just sit there and agree with me.'
> Margaret Thatcher, 1925–

There is a form of public speaking that is a team effort. It is the formal debate, and it is great fun.

Because you are part of a team, speaking in a debate is a little less alarming than trying to prepare a speech on your own. Indeed, a debating team must work together or success is not assured. A team effort in debating is just as important as in sport; each team member is essential to the whole, and each must play a particular part. Like any other team game there are rules to be followed.

The debate is controlled by a chairperson, addressed as 'Madam Chairman' or 'Mr Chairman'. The chairperson also acts as timekeeper.

The winning team is determined by a process of adjudication. A judgement is given by one person, or by a team of adjudicators (three avoids a deadlock). They mark each debater for manner, method and matter, and also for successful rebuttals.

THE PROCEDURE

A subject for debate is given to two teams of three each. The debate is a contest between these two teams as they try to persuade the listeners to accept the proposition they are advancing. The team taking the positive side, that is, arguing *for* the proposition, is known as the **Affirmative**; the team arguing *against* the proposal is known as the **Negative**. The affirmative team sits on the right side of the chairperson and begins the debate. The negative team sits to the left of the chairperson and ends the debate. The team members support each other's arguments and rebut the opposition as often, and as forcefully, as possible.

The first speaker for the Affirmative should define the words used in the topic, outline the team's argument plan, and begin to develop the first arguments.

The first speaker for the Negative agrees or disagrees with the definition of the topic, rebuts any arguments put forward, outlines the team plan and begins to introduce arguments in favour of the negative case.

The second speakers for both the Affirmative and Negative should present the bulk of the new matter for their side of the debate, criticise the opposition's stance, and take every opportunity to enforce their own argument by reasoned rebuttal.

The third speaker for the Affirmative demolishes all arguments brought forward by the opposition, refers to the original case plan, adds to the points already made by the Affirmative, contrasts the two sides of the debate and emphatically sums up the Affirmative's propositions.

The third speaker for the Negative restates the team's aims in the arguments, rebuts everything brought forward by the opposing side and sums up the points brought forward in

support of their side of the debate. This speaker *may not* introduce any new matter and is penalised if this rule is broken.

FLEXIBLE RULES

Debating rules in general are not hard and fast, for initiative in presentation is encouraged, but they are a fine skeleton on which to build the body of any debate. The one rule that may not be broken is the one about new matter being introduced by the third speaker. This is done because the Affirmative side does not have an opportunity to rebut anything brought forward at this final stage.

PLANNING

Preparation time together – the training session if you like – gives each team a chance to discuss the topic fully. Arguments are given to each speaker to flesh out, with the first and third speaker using those arguments in precis. A good debater can construct an argument whether the subject appeals or not, and whether the side allocated suits her or his own viewpoint or not.

These sessions together also give each team a chance to imagine the arguments that will be brought against them and to plan the rebuttals needed to refute those claims. Carefully consider, while you are together, the matter, the manner and the method of your presentation (see Chapter 19).

Then consider the placement of your speakers. Getting that order right is vital. The third speaker must have a quick, argumentative mind, so that speaking at short notice and from scribbled notes (taken as other speakers are declaiming) is a challenge and not a worry. The total time given to previous speakers (and each speaker is given a time limit that must be rigidly adhered to) is all the time the third speaker will have to summon up rebuttals and comments.

THE PLEASURES

Debating is a marvellous way to learn to think, and to speak, 'on your feet'. The cut and thrust of argument is exciting and often rewarding. When a team is successful there is the feeling of success that comes from exercising a skill. Debating is a talent to be fostered and nourished in the same way as the skill of handling the ball is encouraged in a sport. The results can be spectacular.

A DEBATING SOCIETY

If there is no debating society in your area, why not form one yourself? One advertisement in your local paper could bring you into a whole new world, for you will be meeting people of like minds and of similar interests.

Subjects for debate are endless. Your own imagination, the daily press, world events, your local issues, can all be grist to your mill. There are two sides to everything, and discovering those sides in reasoned debate sharpens the mind wonderfully. Try it. As a form of public speaking it is hard to beat ... though that's debatable!

Checklist: debating

- Work as a team
- Establish the rules and observe them
- Understand your individual role as a speaker
- Use preparation time well
- Place speakers in the best order
- Form a debating society
- Look out for new topics

12 USING A MICROPHONE

'The object of oratory alone is not truth, but persuasion.'
Thomas Babington Macaulay, 1800–1859

Happily more people are becoming accustomed to using a microphone in these days of electronic devices. Once it was a most worrying thing to have suspended in front of you. For some people it still is. Don't be one of them.

Remind yourself that the microphone is not there to make you feel nervous. It is there simply as a means of communication – to enable you to be heard all over the hall. It is an aid, and one which you should use if at all possible. Should it prove temperamental (and they often do), make a light-hearted remark about it and move away from it. Pitch your voice to be heard well down the expanse of the hall and thank your lucky rehearsals that you know how.

JUST TESTING

When you are invited to be a speaker, remember to ask if there will be a microphone. If the answer is yes, arrive early at the venue and test it for yourself. Microphones vary almost as much as people do and you cannot take them for granted. If you have friends with you, position them in various parts of the room and ask them to listen to you. Try this with a part of your speech your listeners have never heard, not with well-worn poems or the count to ten. Why? The listeners are expecting to hear seven follow six and so they give a thumbs-up. You must test for the unfamiliar.

If there appears to be some distortion, move back slightly from the microphone or lower it a little. The ideal position for the instrument is just below your chin and eighteen inches away from you, whether you are standing or sitting.

JUDGE THE VOLUME

If it is not possible to make some tests, listen carefully as you are being introduced. As you will probably be behind the amplifiers you won't hear the exact sound the audience does. You need, therefore, to look at the people to gauge their reaction to the amplified voice. If they appear to be straining to hear, you will know that you need to project your own delivery a little more. If they are being blasted out of their seats, ask for the volume to be turned back or, if that is not possible, stand well back from the monster. Alternatively, decide not to use it.

NOISES OFF

Using a microphone is a situation where you must be sure that your notes are small or that your speech (if it *must* be read) is on non-rattling paper. A microphone picks up every sound. Crunching paper sounds as though the building is on fire, so it is to be avoided at all costs. You don't want your audience melting away in panic! Have your notes at a comfortable distance for

your eyes to pick up those trigger words, but below the microphone so that the noise is kept to a minimum.

The same warning applies to chunky jewellery, especially bracelets. Don't wear a bracelet; it is bound to move and the microphone will make it sound like thunder. If you have a pen or pencil with you, don't tap it on the lectern. If it is a ballpoint pen, don't punch the spring constantly. This will sound like a machine-gun and will distract the listeners to screaming point.

Indeed with a microphone in front of you, you must keep your mannerisms under control. If you are an arm-waver you are likely to hit the sensitive thing, and send a dreadful blasting noise through the auditorium.

Don't hold your notes up between you and the microphone: not only will this create a barrier to your eye rapport, but it will also act as a baffle to the passage of air between your mouth and the microphone. You might as well wrap your head up in a blanket. It will have the same effect.

KEEP STILL

The microphone cannot follow you around (unless you have been fitted with a high-tech throat mike, and they are so expensive it is unlikely to be the case), so be careful to stand or sit still. As you have made certain that the microphone is at your correct level, you will still be able to project your personality above it and your smiles will still be seen. Try not to turn your head too far away from it, for your choice words will be lost if you do. Try not to drop your chin too much or consult those notes too much, for the same loss will be experienced.

There are physical restrictions imposed on you when you are using a microphone, but you must train yourself to be comfortable with them. Only when you are happy with your use of the microphone can you relax and be yourself. Of course you have to adapt to its needs, but you need not be a slave to it.

THE DUMMY RUN

Standing or sitting still is a position of necessity so that you can communicate more fully and more easily. Practise at home until you no longer feel 'frozen'. Rig up something in front of you that can be a microphone for your purposes, set your notes before you, and deliver your speech. Stay within the confines you have set yourself and work at it until you are totally relaxed. If you kick or brush against the 'mike', you have definitely strayed too far and have something to correct at your rehearsals.

The more familiar you become with the use of these temperamental electronic gadgets, the better your public performances will be. And that's the aim always: to improve.

BE AWARE

Stay mindful of the fact that you are addressing an audience, even though you have that mechanical device between you. Don't fall into the trap of addressing the microphone itself. It is there only as a means to an end. It is not the focus of your speech.

Look over it and beyond it to establish that eye rapport. Don't hold it or lean on it, and don't take it into your confidence.

Be aware that you are the speaker and that the microphone is only a further projection for your voice. Your eyes, your expressive face and your (restrained) gestures are still important. In fact when you use a microphone they are *more* important. Your personality has to come across to your listeners despite that artificial aid, so you may have to work a little harder at that aspect. You cannot move about or alter your stance too dramatically, so your manner and your rapport with your audience is crucial. Vary your delivery as much as you can to make it even more interesting. Ignore the microphone, be yourself, and success is assured.

Checklist: using a microphone

- A microphone is a further means of communication
- Check the microphone before you begin to speak
- Watch for noisy objects near the device
- Don't wear jangling jewellery
- Don't play with your pen or spectacles
- Position your notes carefully
- Remember to stay within the microphone's range
- Practise with a dummy mike
- Project your personality beyond the microphone

13 SPEAKING ON RADIO

Journalist: 'Didn't you have anything on?'
Marilyn Monroe: 'I had the radio on.'

Being asked to speak or to be interviewed on radio or television can be a daunting prospect – if you let it take over. When it happens, view it as yet another extension of yourself and of the work you have been doing to teach yourself to speak in public. This time your public will be infinitely more varied and somewhat greater in numbers, but that is really the only difference. The trick for both speaking in public and speaking on radio or television is never to think that you are speaking to thousands, but to concentrate your mind on that *one* person out there to whom you are addressing your remarks. That person is deeply interested in what you are saying, and you want to keep it that way. Speak to, and not at, that listener and all will be well.

THE SET-UP

A radio station is much less intimidating than a television station. The set-up is much simpler. Usually it is you, your interviewer, a producer (if you're lucky) and a control-booth operator. You and your interviewer will be at a desk or table with a microphone between you. The formula is to have a chat in as relaxed a manner as possible.

THE QUESTIONS

You may be lucky enough to see a list of questions beforehand. You can always ask for a list so that you will have some idea of the direction the questions will take; for example you need to know if the interviewer is likely to be confrontational.

WHY YOU?

Perhaps the most important question is yours when you are asked to be interviewed or to take part in a discussion: the question is 'Why?'. If you know why you have been asked you will be able to predict the direction of the questions that will come your way. If you are violently opposed to building a new motorway and have gone public on the matter and the discussion is to be about this issue, it is easy to understand why you have been asked to participate. If the reason isn't obvious, find out.

THE ANSWERS

Whatever the subject, think of the curliest questions and work out desirable answers. You will thus be prepared for anything the interviewer or panel member can fire in your direction.

Try to keep your answers short and to the point. There never seems to be enough time allowed for interviews, so you need to take advantage of the small amount allowed to you. Don't repeat questions; this takes up valuable seconds. Give your answers quickly and crisply. Make your points in the same fashion and you will be amazed at how much you *can* say in the short time.

THINK BEFORE YOU ACCEPT

Though radio is a less complicated medium than television, don't take it for granted. You need to think at length before you accept any invitation to appear before such a wide audience. You need to discover to your own satisfaction whether what you have to contribute to any particular subject is relevant and valuable. If you cannot be confident of your contribution, turn down the invitation; you will not have lost anything.

YOUR PERFORMANCE

In radio you do not have any props to assist you. Your voice and your voice alone is your instrument for communication. If you are sharing your views on home cookery, for example, you cannot have luscious shots of mouth-watering food to help your descriptions. Everything depends on you.

It is up to you to cut out 'ums' and 'ers' from your speech. They really do sound unprofessional on radio. Find the word you want and use it without that nervous I-am-not-sure-what-to-say-next reaction. In ordinary speech and conversation it doesn't really matter too much, but it certainly matters on fast-moving radio.

Quick thinking is required, especially if you have a sharp interviewer. Don't let that microphone sap your confidence and don't let the interviewer go off at a tangent. If a question is asked that you think is not germane to the topic, answer it with something like 'May I say this first ...' or 'The main issue surely is ...' It is *your* interview and you have been asked to express a point of view. If the interviewer moves away from the subject you have every right to bring her or him back to it.

THE RADIO TALK

Giving a talk on radio, as distinct from being interviewed, is less common now than it was some years ago although it still does occur. If such an opportunity comes your way, grasp it. In this instance you will have the script before you and as it will have been written by you it produces no threat at all; you can enjoy it.

The talk will probably be pre-recorded, so if you mess it up the first time round it can be re-done. The producer will give you tips on how to improve your delivery. The technician will have taken a voice-level check, so you don't have to worry about the placement of the microphone.

A piece of cake? Yes, it really is, but you still need to deliver this radio talk in your best possible manner, with as much light and shade and expression as you can muster. You need to interest your listeners from the first few words, as in any ordinary speech, and you need to leave them with much food for thought. Remember always that it is possible to switch off a radio, and you don't want that happening to you and your well-prepared talk!

Checklist: speaking on radio

- Radio is another extension of public speaking
- Always find out why you have been asked
- Ask for a list of questions
- Keep your answers short and to the point
- Your voice is the only means of communication you will have
- Control the interviewer
- Make yourself interesting for listeners

14 SPEAKING ON TELEVISION

'Television? No good will come of this device.
The word is half Greek and half Latin.'
C.P. Scott, 1846–1932

~~~~~~

Speaking on television is a little more nerve-racking than speaking on radio, mainly because of all the equipment needed to get you to the screen. It can be overwhelming. Don't be engulfed by it. You have been asked to participate, so the station personnel have confidence in your ability to contribute to the discussion or interview. Grab some of that confidence for yourself, and tell yourself that you will rise to this challenge as to all others.

YOUR SURROUNDINGS

Arrive a little early so that you can familiarise yourself with the surroundings. Cameras, sets, microphones, people milling everywhere and strange jargon can all be intimidating the first time round.

Your producer will tell you where to sit and will give you a throat mike or tell you that the overhead microphone will be positioned correctly for your voice. A check will be done to ensure that all is well, and adjustments will be made. You don't have to be troubled about these technical matters.

PREPARING AND PRESENTING

If you have been provided beforehand with a list of likely questions, think carefully about your answers. Time is vitally important in television, so to get the most out of it you must be clear and succinct in all your statements.

If, for example, you are there to promote a forthcoming amateur musical production, it is useless to waffle about past performances and players, leaving yourself no time to enthuse about the present. Keep strictly to the point, and look at the questioner. You will feel more confident with this face-to-face talk because you have established eye rapport and can bounce off the personality of the interviewer, as well as exerting your own. The cameras will follow you, so you do not need to speak with your neck twisted round towards the lens. Be as relaxed as you can, for you will then appear comfortable to the viewers, who might be persuaded to leave their sets switched on.

THE INTERVIEW

With the very first questions try to sound positive. Whatever else you do, *don't* begin your answer with 'Well ... er', 'I think ...' or 'Maybe ...' Even if you are not absolutely certain, sound as though you are. This will capture the interest of the audience more readily than anything else, for they will find you credible. In television, where there are many distractions, this is most important.

Ignore the heat of the lights, ignore the camera, concentrate on the presenter or the other panel members and you will be assessed as 'good talent'.

YOUR APPEARANCE

Your appearance must be a little more up-market than when you appear an radio, where old jeans and a grubby T-shirt may be acceptable. At least your T-shirt should be clean! Once you have decided on your outfit, forget it. It is no good fussing at the last moment about a crinkled collar or spotty tie; nothing can be done then. Just check your own appearance before you leave home and be satisfied with it. The make-up department will attend to your face. Relax and let them do it. They know what is best for the probing eye of the camera and will match any colours necessary to your skin type, or clothing.

Most of us are very conscious of how we appear to others and are conscious too of how critical we have been of how others look on television. This makes us more nervous of our appearance than of our performance. It ought to be the reverse: what you say is far more important than how you look while saying it. Work on that and, once happy with your appearance, forget it completely and think your way into the interview.

USE THE QUESTIONS

Mentally alert yourself to the points you want to put over. That is why you are there. Such opportunities come but rarely and you should make the most of them, whatever the reason for your appearance. Three or four points are possibly all that time will allow you to cover, so fix those firmly in your mind.

If you are quick-thinking you will be able to turn a question around to suit your purposes or those of the group you are representing. For example, to an interviewer asking, 'Do you expect to influence the hospital board?' you might reply, 'Not really. We are there to raise money to help the hospital in all its endeavours. The board governs, we need to raise a million dollars so that the board can continue. That's the purpose of our special gold lottery'.

CLEVER ANSWERS

Keep your answers as short as possible. In that way more questions will be asked and you will have more opportunities to cover more ground. Don't repeat the question as you often hear people doing on both radio and television. That wastes seconds, and they all add up. Television is a voracious monster. It gobbles up material endlessly. The moment you have finished, on will come something completely different. Leave your viewers with at least one point to ponder so that 'Fish in Alaska', or whatever the next topic is, does not linger in their minds long enough to take precedence over your matter.

You do not have a chance to wind up the interview yourself. The presenter will do that – and sometimes while you are mid-sentence – because time is up. That is why every statement ought to be relevant and ought to be a winner.

The nerves you might have suffered initially will give way as you begin to enjoy the experience. It's quite a thrill to appear on television, however briefly, and you ought to enjoy it.

Checklist: speaking on television

- The studio is confident you can contribute
- Ask beforehand for questions or direction of the interview
- The camera follows you, not the reverse
- Be positive in your approach
- Be comfortable with your appearance
- Time will be in short supply
- Keep strictly to the point
- Short answers ensure more questions
- The timing is the responsibility of the presenter

---

15 THE MEDIUM AND THE MESSAGE

'To me the need to talk is a primary impulse, and I can't help
saying right off what comes to my tongue.'
Miguel de Cervantes, 1547–1616

When you are asked to become part of a radio or television
programme, make certain you know the answers to the questions
below. With this knowledge your fears will disappear and you
will be able to project yourself, but not as that apprehensive
wreck you thought you would be by the time the day rolled
round.

■ Why have I been asked?
■ What type of programme is it?
■ Will it be live or 1 re-recorded?
■ Who is the interv wer/presenter/chairperson?
■ What is the time limit?
■ Am I the only guest, or is it a discussion panel?
■ Is it likely to be pro- or anti- my viewpoint?
■ May I see the questions in advance?
■ If not the exact questions, may I know the line of questioning?
■ If recorded will it be edited?

If you know why you have been asked you can correct from
the outset any wrong assumption about your view. Knowing
the type of programme gives you a chance to listen to or look at
some similar shows so that you know what to expect. If a

programme is to be recorded, you know that some re-takes are possible. If live, you are on your mettle from the first moment. Once you know who is to be in charge of the session you can learn something of the techniques that she or he uses, and prepare yourself. Knowing the time limit gives you a chance to trim your thoughts to this constraint. If you are one of a panel there is not so much pressure upon you and that knowledge is relaxing.

KNOWING THE QUESTIONS IN ADVANCE

Even if the programme is likely to be violently against your stance on the topic, you can prepare for an attack if you know something about the questions beforehand. If the bias of the questioner shows clearly, the interviewee gains by comparison. The questions, or the line of questioning, give you an idea of how to tackle the answers. (Do not rehearse your answers. An interview must sound spontaneous to be believed.)

THE EDITED INTERVIEW

If you know that the talk or interview or discussion is to be edited you can defend yourself easily if you feel the tape has been tampered with to change the essence of what was actually said. Usually editing is done to bring a segment back to its time limit or to remove something that might land you or the station in political – or legal – hot water.

UNDERSTANDING THE MEDIUM

Public speaking that gives you an audience of thousands is to be welcomed but it is ephemeral. Because of the nature of the beast you really must prepare so that your points are made, and made well, while on air. It is useless to chastise yourself later; the moment has come and gone and you may not be given another opportunity. Be a well-prepared scout: think ahead, plan ahead, know your topic thoroughly and then speak your mind. You will know when you have employed your information and the medium to the best of your practised ability, and it's a great feeling.

An invitation to appear on radio or television is a chance for you to use the medium – not for it to use you. Remember that and you really will be triumphant!

Checklist: the medium and the message

■ Consider the questions in advance
■ Don't rehearse your answers
■ Grasp the opportunity
■ Don't allow the medium to use you – use it instead

---

16 FORMS OF ADDRESS

'... First Lord of the Treasury, Lord Chief Justice,
Commander-in-Chief, Lord High Admiral, Master of the
Buckhounds, Groom of the Back Stairs, Archbishop of Titipu,
and Lord Mayor, both acting and elect, all rolled into one.'

W.S. Gilbert, 1836–1911

For everything except the most informal of speeches you need to address your hosts and distinguished guests before you begin. It is important to know the correct forms of address for such dignitaries. To help you, here are some forms of address you are likely to encounter.

THE CHAIR

The person in the chair is the first person you mention: 'Madam Chairman' or 'Mr Chairman'. Some organisations may have agreed to use another form, so check beforehand. If the president of an organisation is in the chair it is permissible to say 'Madam President' or 'Mr President'.

BRITISH ROYALS AND PEERS

The Queen and the Queen Mother are 'Your Majesty'. On the first occasion you address them directly in your speech you

again say 'Your Majesty', but on subsequent occasions you say 'Ma'am'.

A prince or a royal duke is addressed as 'Your Royal Highness'. On the first occasion you address him directly in your speech you again say 'Your Royal Highness', but on subsequent occasions you say 'Sir'.

A princess or a duchess is addressed as 'Your Royal Highness' as for a prince, but is then addressed as 'Ma'am'.

For members of the British peerage, a duke is 'My Lord Duke' or 'Your Grace'; a marquess is 'My Lord Marquess'; an earl, viscount or baron is 'My Lord'; a duchess is 'Your Grace'; and a Marchioness, Countess or Viscountess or Baroness is 'My Lady'.

CHURCH AND STATE

A Dame or a Knight of the realm may be an official guest. If this is the case the full forms of address are 'Dame Lucy Roser' and 'Sir Robert Lee', but if you need to address them directly later on, they are just 'Dame Lucy' and 'Sir Robert'.

The Prime Minister might be there; he or she is 'Mr (or Madam) Prime Minister', or 'Prime Minister'.

A minister of the Crown is addressed as 'Madam (or Mr) Minister' (or simply as 'Sir' if male).

A Governor-General is 'Your Excellency' and his wife (or her husband) is also entitled to this form of address. State governors are addressed as 'Your Excellency', but their wives or husbands are addressed by their normal title.

A rabbi is 'Rabbi'; an archbishop 'Your Grace'; a bishop 'My Lord'; a dean 'Mr Dean'; an archdeacon 'Mr Archdeacon' or 'Archdeacon'; a rector or priest 'Father'; and a minister of religion 'The Reverend Mr' (or Ms, Miss or Mrs).

An ambassador is 'Your Excellency'.

LORD MAYORS AND MAYORS

The lord mayors of Belfast, Cardiff, Dublin, London and York, whether male or female, are addressed as 'My Lord'. A lady mayoress (usually the wife of the lord mayor, but occasionally a partner, daughter, mother or sister) is addressed as 'My Lady'. A mayor of a city or borough, again whether male or female, is 'Your Worship' or 'Mr Mayor'. The wife of a mayor is addressed as 'Mayoress', never 'Your Worship'. The husband or partner of a female mayor bears no title (unless, of course, he has one in his own right).

THE LAW

Judges of the High Court are usually knighted or made Dame of the Most Excellent Order of the British Empire when they are appointed and are addressed and referred to as 'My Lord' and 'His Lordship' or 'My Lady' and 'Her Ladyship' on the Bench and in the precincts of the Court. In their private capacities, however, they may be addressed as 'Mr/Mrs Justice —', 'Judge —', 'Sir —' or

'Dame — —'. Circuit judges are addressed and referred to on the Bench as 'Your Honour' and 'His Honour'; socially they are addressed as 'Judge' or 'Judge —'.

DO YOUR HOMEWORK AND FEEL CONFIDENT

If you are in the situation where you will be called upon to give a speech in front of such luminaries, you should do your homework and know the correct forms of address. *Always* check before you speak, and write them down in your notes. It is part of lessening your panic and soothing your nerves. You know you are right, so you can relax.

Checklist: forms of address

■ How to address dignitaries
■ Chairperson
■ Titled people
■ Church and state
■ Lord mayors and mayors
■ The law

17 BAD SPEECHES

'No one ever seems to listen to what he says, and even after five minutes he gives the impression that, since he started speaking, amoebas have evolved into vertebrates, crawled out of the ocean, stood upright and invented the wheel and the atom bomb.'

Mungo Wentworth MacCallum, 1941–

Can you imagine a better description for a boring speaker than this one? Don't let it happen to you.

THE LAZY INTRODUCTION

We have all been at a function where the introduction of the guest speaker is merely: 'Mr Stan Sleger needs no introduction. We all know him. Mr Sleger'. Nothing could be worse and yet it happens constantly. Even if Stan is the best-known person in the world it is discourteous not to introduce him properly. Apart from that, there could be some members of the audience who, while having heard the Sleger name on numerous occasions, have no idea why he has been asked to speak this time. They have the right to be informed by the introductory address.

THAT TIRED FIRST PHRASE

'Unaccustomed as I am to public speaking' is about the very worst beginning for a speech. If it is your very first time on your feet before a group of people, they don't want to know that and you don't want to admit it. Some wit is bound to say that it was obvious anyway! That tired phrase has been around for years, and you should not help perpetuate it.

THE SUPERFLUOUS REMARK

Then there is the bore who uses long words strung together in meaningless phrases. 'I'm sure I speak for all of us' means 'we'; use that instead. 'On this never-to-be forgotten occasion I rise to my feet in answer to your invitation to address you on the subject of how to speak in public.' The audience has dozed off already. Besides, no speaker worthy of the name would announce the theme of the speech. The snappy first few words give that away, without a thunderous announcement to that effect.

'It gives me enormous pleasure' surely means 'I am glad': try to keep it simple and sincere. 'This point in time' is 'now'! Also on the banned list is, 'I don't know what I can say to add to what the other speakers have said'. Of course you are about to say something, or you would not be on your feet. Just begin. You don't need that apologetic little hook. It could be translated as, 'Don't bother listening to me, I have nothing to say'.

STATISTICS THAT KILL

'Did you know that there are 10,283 cogs in this machine and that each one cost £14.23 and took 17.2478 person-hours to install?' Statistics, statistics! Who needs them? No one will remember those figures, so they ought not to be used. Instead of this deadening sentence, what about: 'Did you know there are over 10,000 cogs in this machine, and each took nearly 18 hours to install?'. Some of that might stick in the listeners' minds and it is a surprising opening to your speech, for such figures are generally not known.

JOKES, QUOTES AND ANECDOTES

'There was an Irishman, an Englishman and a Scotsman ...' What a done-to-death beginning! It usually has nothing to do with the subject of the talk and is equally objectionable when it is heard in the body of the speech.

A string of jokes, however harmless, may entertain for a short time, but will not hold the interest of your listeners unless you are a gifted, stand-up comic.

We have all heard a speaker who constantly says, 'That reminds me ...' and then launches into a rambling personal story that touches on the theme of the speech but adds nothing. One anecdote after another is as numbing as one joke after another. An occasional illuminating personal or family experience will add substance, but not a string of them. Be aware of this trap.

Along with the string of anecdotes comes the string of quotations. One after the other they are tedious. You are showing off knowledge, but no one except yourself is interested. A few to support your case are acceptable, a constant stream is not. Beware!

DISTRACTIONS

You have only to watch people on television to understand annoying mannerisms. These can be in use of words or in gesture. Try to learn from bad example. Perhaps the most maddening is the use of 'you know ...' between sentences and often between words. It's a device to allow the brain a little more time to think, but it drives a listener crazy. Similarly, a flip of the head or a sweep of the arm used too frequently can ruin an otherwise appealing speech. Rehearse in front of a mirror, and that will force you to change. You'll worry yourself.

DROPPING NAMES

Perhaps the worst speaker of all is the one who is a big-noter. 'I did this ... I did that', 'My friend Lady Mariette ...', 'When I was in Morocco ...', 'When I was shopping in Harrods ...' We all know the type. From a public platform it is a disaster. No audience wants to be treated to this load of personal reminiscences, most of which have probably been exaggerated for the occasion. One apt, truthful narrative is a different matter.

The use of 'I' must be watched, and eliminated as much as possible. Needless to say, 'I, personally, myself' is a tautology not to be tolerated.

Checklist: bad speeches

- Never ignore the need to introduce
- Some stale, worn-out beginnings for speeches
- Talking just for the sake of it
- Avoid statistics
- You are a speaker, not a comedian
- Check for annoying mannerisms
- Don't be an egotist

18 GOOD SPEECHES

'Talking and eloquence are not the same:
to speak, and to speak well, are two things.'
Ben Jonson, 1573–1637

~~~~~~~~~~~~~~~~~~~~~~~~~~~~~~~~~~

Essentially a good speech is one that leaves the audience wanting more. The good speaker can recognise when this moment is imminent and will finish the address.

FIRST-SENTENCE IMPACT

A speech that begins with a startling comment – 'I am about to argue with a definition in the Encyclopaedia Brittanica', 'It's impossible to put the toothpaste back into the tube', or 'Women are people too' – will always gain attention. So will 'Listen carefully' or 'What do you think?'. The variations are limitless, but you must think of something yourself or you are doomed from the beginning.

SHORT AND PITHY

A speech that is scheduled for fifteen minutes and takes fourteen minutes is always popular, particularly if the speaker has actually had something to say during those moments.

An address that gives the audience something to mull over and to discuss for some time afterwards is one that has had an impact. Don't be afraid to be controversial so long as you have some facts to support your premise. Some of the finest speakers are those who have encouraged us to think or do. Winston Churchill was a splendid example of that. His World War 2 speeches were universally uplifting, thoughtful and encouraging. They were carefully rehearsed but sounded spontaneous – another mark of a good speaker.

INVOLVE YOUR AUDIENCE

A speech that involves the audience in some way is one respected and liked too; sharing some aspect of your speech directly with the people you are addressing makes them feel special.

If you are speaking to an audience of engineers it is not appropriate to show them examples of craftwork, as it would be to a group arranging a fund-raising fete, but there will be something that you *can* share.

It is usually possible to build this in at the planning stage, but it may also be workable while you are making your remarks. If the introduction has included, for example, a comment about your work that you can enlarge upon with some relevance to your engineers or fund-raisers, do that.

If you become aware of something about the town or city where you are speaking, add that somewhere along the track. This signals to your audience that you are really aware of them as citizens of that area, and that there is something in your address especially for them.

CONCLUDE WITH A FLOURISH

Always the speech that concludes with a ringing statement is the memorable one. You want to be remembered; that is why you took so much time and trouble with your thoughts, so don't let yourself down with a limp ending or lame thanks.

Indicate that your comments have concluded by summing up your arguments with an emphatic few words. Know that sentence by heart so that you can look at your audience, smile at them, embrace them with your glance, make them feel part of the action. Pause for a moment or two to allow your listeners to evaluate fully what you have just said. Step back from the rostrum. Wait for the stunning applause!

Checklist: good speeches

- Leave your audience wanting more
- Don't be afraid to be controversial
- Have some facts to support your argument
- Involve your audience in some personal way
- No lame endings allowed!
- Wait for the applause

19 FROM THEORY TO PRACTICE

'The only place where success comes before work is a dictionary.'
Vidal Sassoon, 1928–

~~~~~~~~~~~~~~~~~~~~~~~~~~

Having read as far as this you are now ready to put all this theory into practice. You are ready to accept every chance that comes your way to speak in public. This is precisely what you must do. Accept every invitation. From moving a motion at your tennis club to addressing a conference of a thousand people, you are prepared for every challenge. This is the way to learn. It is akin to diving into the deep end of the pool, but there is no other way. Your practice in front of your mirror at home is not enough. The skill is, after all, called speaking in *public*, and it has to be pursued in public. You will be surprised at how quickly you become accustomed to speaking aloud and you'll be delighted with the response you receive from your audience, two or two hundred. The better you become the warmer will be the reaction. It's a good feeling.

A SPEAKER'S SUMMARY

Here is a summary for you. If you remember this 'M and P' list you will become a well-prepared, confident speaker and you will most certainly be in demand.

Be mindful of:

- **Matter** – material, facts, sources of information, insight. Keep it simple, relevant and accurate.
- **Manner** – logic, success in communicating, persuasiveness, sympathy with audience. Keep it friendly and sincere.
- **Method** – organisation of the speech itself, ingenuity in presentation and attack. Keep it grammatical and exact.

Be persuaded by:

- **Preparation** – essential, no matter how experienced you become.
- **Practice** – vital to every speaker.
- **Pace** – keep your delivery slow enough for your audience to follow you.
- **Pauses** – use them well, to allow your audience to take in what you are saying and for dramatic effect.
- **Pitch** – is necessary for your voice to carry. Project your voice so that you are heard easily.
- **Punch** – your delivery needs it to deliver your conviction and carry your argument. Punch comes into its own when you utter your final sentence.

So there you are – a public speaker, ready to speak in public! Your dedicated work has brought you success.

Checklist: from theory to practice

- Accept all invitations to speak in public
- Remember your M and P list for success:
  - Matter, Manner and Method
  - Preparation, Practice, Pace, Pauses, Pitch and Punch

OTHER TITLES IN THE SERIES

Tips and Techniques for Microwave Cooking
How to Remove Stains
How to Make Over 200 Cocktails
Choosing Baby Names
Chess Made Easy
Family First Aid
Choosing Dog Names
Choosing Cat Names
The Pocket Easy Speller